The Unification of Italy

The Unification of Italy

John Gooch

R

ROUTLEDGE · LONDON

First published in 1986 by
Methuen & Co. Ltd

Reprinted 1989 by
Routledge
11 New Fetter Lane
London EC4P 4EE

© 1986 John Gooch

Typeset in Great Britain by
Scarborough Typesetting Services
and printed by
Richard Clay Ltd, Bungay, Suffolk

British Library Cataloguing in Publication Data

Gooch, John
The unification of Italy.
– (Lancaster pamphlets)
1. Italy – History –
1849–1870
I. Title   II. Series
945'.08   DG552

ISBN 0–415–04595–9

Contents

Foreword

Lancaster Pamphlets offer concise and up-to-date accounts of major historical topics, primarily for the help of students preparing for Advanced Level examinations, though they should also be of value to those pursuing introductory courses in universities and other institutions of higher education. They do not rely on prior textbook knowledge. Without being all-embracing, their aims are to bring some of the central themes or problems confronting students and teachers into sharper focus than the textbook writer can hope to do; to provide the reader with some of the results of recent research which the textbook may not embody; and to stimulate thought about the whole interpretation of the topic under discussion. At the end of this pamphlet is a list of the recent or fairly recent works that the writer considers most relevant to the subject.

Time chart

Year	Piedmont	Kingdom of the Two Sicilies	Papal States
1807		Foundation of Carbonari	
1814–15			
1820		Revolution (July)	
1821	Revolution (March), bringing abdication of Victor Emmanuel I, crushed by Charles Felix (d. 1831) and Austrians (April–Oct.)		
1830			
1831	Accession of Charles Albert		Revolutions put down by Austrians (Feb.–March)
1832			
1834	Mazzini fails in invasion of Savoy (Feb.)		
1837		Risings fail	
1843			Risings fail
1844			Rising by Bandiera brothers fails (June)
1846			
1847			Civic guard formed in Rome; Austrians occupy Ferrara (July)

Year	The Duchies	Lombardy	Venetia	General
1807				
1814–15				Congress of Vienna
1820				
1821				Congress of Laibach (opens 26 Jan.)
1830				Death of pope Pius VIII (30 Nov.)
1831	Revolutions in Parma and Modena put down by Austrians (Feb.)			Election of pope Gregory XVI (2 Feb.)
1832				Mazzini (1805–72) founds *Young Italy*
1834				
1837				
1843				
1844				
1846				Election of pope Pius IX (16 June)
1847		Riots suppressed (Sept.)		Italy struck by economic crisis (autumn)

Year	Piedmont	Kingdom of the Two Sicilies	Papal States
1848	Draft constitution announced (8 Feb.); Charles Albert declares war against Austrians (26 March); Piedmontese defeated by Austrians at Custozza (25 July); armistice with Austria (10 Aug.)	Risings (Jan.); provisional government in Sicily declares Ferdinand II and his dynasty permanently deposed (13 April); Ferdinand dissolves assembly and national guard in Naples (17 May)	Demonstration against new ministry (1 Jan.); pope grants constitution (13 March); pope announces he has no temporal ambitions (29 April); pope flees (24 Nov.)
1849	Resumption of war with Austria (20 March); Piedmontese defeated at Novara (23 March), and Charles Albert abdicates, his successor being Victor Emmanuel II (d. 1878); armistice (26 March); peace of Milan (6 Aug.)	Recapture of Sicily begins (29 March); Palermo recaptured (15 April)	Popular assembly declares Rome a republic (10 Feb.); Austrians reoccupy Ferrara (8 Feb.); French troops land at Civitavecchia (24 April); French take Rome (2 July)
1850	Cavour (1810–61) becomes minister		Pius IX returns to Rome (12 April)
1852	Cavour becomes premier (4 Nov.)		
1855	Piedmont joins Crimean War against Russia (26 Jan.)		
1856	Cavour at Congress of Paris		
1857		Failure of invasion of Sicily by Pisacane (1 July)	

Year	The Duchies	Lombardy	Venetia	General
1848	Austrians occupy Parma and Modena (Jan.); draft constitution announced in Tuscany (15 Feb.)	'No smoking' protest begins in Milan (1 Jan.); Austrians and police kill demonstrators (3 Jan.); 'glorious five days' (18–23 March) in Milan; plebiscite votes for fusion with Piedmont (8 June); Austrians seize Milan (5 Aug.)	Successful revolution against Austrians in Venice (22 March)	Year of Revolutions
1849	Austrians restore ruler of Tuscany (28 July)		Venice capitulates to Austrians (27 Aug.)	
1850				
1852	Constitution abolished in Tuscany (6 May)			
1855	Austrians leave Tuscany			
1856				
1857				Pallavicino founds Italian National Society

Year	Piedmont	Kingdom of the Two Sicilies	Papal States
1858	Pack of Plombières with Napoleon III (20 July)		
1859	Alliance with France (26 Jan.); Austrian ultimatum to Piedmont (23 April); war with Austria (29 April); Austrians defeated by French and Piedmontese at Magenta (4 June), by French at Solferino (24 June) and by Piedmontese at San Martino (24 June); armistice between Austria and France (8 July), preceding peace of Villafranca (11 July), which gains Lombardy for Piedmont; Cavour resigns (12 July)		
1860	Cavour returns to office (20 Jan); incorporation of duchies (March); cession of Savoy and Nice to France (1 April)	Unrest in Sicily (April) precedes landing by Garibaldi (1807–82) at Marsala (10 May); Garibaldi takes island in name of Victor Emmanuel, crosses to mainland (18 Aug), enters Naples (7 Sept) and wins battle of the Volturno (1 Oct.); Garibaldi hands regions over to Victor Emmanuel at Teano (26 Oct)	Patriots vote for incorporation into Piedmont (March); risings (8 Sept.); Piedmontese troops occupy all but Rome (11–29 Sept.), winning battle of Castelfidardo (18 Sept.)

Year	The Duchies	Lombardy	Venetia	General
1858				Orsini attempts to assassinate Napoleon III (14 Jan.)
1859	Rulers of Tuscany, Parma and Modena flee after revolutions (April–May); assembly in Tuscany votes to join Piedmont (20 Aug.)			
1860	Duchies vote to join Piedmont and are incorporated (March)			

Year	Kingdom of Italy

1861
17 Mar.   King Victor Emmanuel II adopts title 'King of Italy'

1862
29 Aug.   Italian troops stop Garibaldi's move on Rome at Aspromonte

1866
18 April   Italy allies with Prussia

20 June   Italy at war with Austria

24 June   Italian army beaten at Custozza

20 July   Italian navy beaten at Lissa

3 Oct.   Peace of Vienna: Austria cedes Venetia to Italy

1867
3 Nov.   Garibaldi defeated by French at Mentana

1870
19 July   Outbreak of Franco–Prussian war

20 Sept.   Italian troops occupy Rome

The Unification of Italy

The Unification of Italy

Introduction

In 1815 Italy consisted of eight separate states. Most were under the direct or indirect control of Austria, and those that were not were ruled by conservative, absolutist kings. Forty-five years later Piedmont–Sardinia, by no stretch of the imagination powerful enough at the outset to dominate the peninsula, provided Italy with her first king and stamped unification on the country. To achieve this foreign domination had to be overcome, local absolute rulers had to be unseated, and the different enthusiasms of patriots had to be united in support of a small, conservative state which occupied only the north-eastern corner of the country and whose upper classes habitually spoke French and not Italian. All this had to be accomplished without stirring the Great Powers, accustomed since the fifteenth century to regarding Italy as their playground, into repressive intervention. In the circumstances it is small wonder that after unification had been achieved Gladstone described it as 'among the greatest marvels of our time'.

The Risorgimento, the movement for the unification of Italy, was seen by contemporaries as a triumph of nationalism – the dominant force of mid-nineteenth-century Europe. To assess how accurate this judgement is, it is necessary to disentangle the many threads which made up Italy's 'national revolution'; for the Risorgimento was in essence a process during which many struggles came together to become one. At its heart lay two

1

motive forces. The first was a search for political liberty within Italy. Those who fought for this goal spread along a spectrum extending from the bourgeoisie, who wanted only to reform and limit the powers of absolutist monarchs, to democrats such as Garibaldi who desired mass involvement in politics. The second force was the search for independence. The desire to cast off oppressive foreign rule ultimately united those directly under Austria's thumb, those whose rulers depended upon Austrian bayonets to sustain them, and those who sought to free themselves from the rule of 'foreign' Italian princes.

The parties involved in each of these struggles – and they were of course often related – were by no means in agreement about their objectives. And it was never a foregone conclusion that they would only be resolved by creating a united Italy. The history of the Risorgimento is the story of how and why these many groups at first struggled separately and failed, and then struggled together and succeeded.

Strands of Revolution, 1815–48

During the first stage of the Risorgimento, men of action put their faith in techniques of revolt to topple unpopular monarchs. Their methods – conspiracy and insurrection – failed. Yet this failure contributed to the long-term success of the Risorgimento, for it helped, first, to demonstrate that to spark off a revolt it was not enough merely to recruit a small, dedicated group of fighters and hope that others would follow their example; some commonly accepted ideological basis was needed to unite men. Secondly, and equally as important, the failures of activists and the quiet success of businessmen and writers contributed to a growing consciousness of national identity. Without this there could have been no 'national' revolution. As yet, however, ideas and action were the concerns of only a very few.

THE NAPOLEONIC LEGACY

From 1796 until 1815 Italy was under French domination. After 1815 the period of French control provided patriots with an important legacy. Left-wing activists could look back with nostalgia to the republic established at Rome in February 1798, to the two Cisalpine republics of the north created in 1797 and 1800 and to the Parthenopean republic proclaimed at Naples in 1799. Monarchists could point to the kingdom of Italy and the kingdom of Naples established in the later years of French domination. Also the efficiency of French government offered a striking contrast to absolutist rule. However, the most important consequence of French rule was to establish in men's minds the idea that Italy could become a unitary state.

BUONARROTI AND THE CARBONARI

For more than a decade after the Restoration of the monarchy secret societies plotted against absolutist rulers. In northern Italy the League of Sublime and Perfect Masters, founded in 1818 and led by Filippo Buonarroti, spread conspiracy from its headquarters in Turin. Its immediate goal was independence from Austria, its ultimate aim – revealed only to a few – was a communistic society. In the kingdom of the Two Sicilies its counterpart was the Carbonari (named after the rural charcoal burners), which had existed in Naples since 1807 and whose chief target was the Church.

In the south the Carbonari joined a rising by elements of the Bourbon army on the night of 1/2 July 1820. Ferdinand quickly gave way and granted a version of the radical Spanish constitution of 1812 – which had a single elective chamber – and at once found himself faced with a separatist rising in Sicily. At the congress of Laibach on 26 January 1821 Ferdinand obtained European support, and with Vienna's assistance he crushed the rebels at the battle of Rieti on 7 March 1821.

In Piedmont, liberal aristocrats and bourgeois democrats plotted to introduce a constitutional régime and unite the province with Lombardy and Venetia in a kingdom of Upper Italy. Revolution broke out on the night of 9/10 March and king Victor Emmanuel I at once abdicated in favour of his brother Charles Felix. Austria, Russia and Prussia would not accept a Piedmontese constitution and Charles Felix flatly refused to have

3

anything to do with it. With Austrian help he easily suppressed the rebels.

The revolutions of 1820–1 had unseated kings in Turin and Naples with apparent ease. However, they had equally easily been crushed by Austrian intervention, underlining the importance of Great Power reaction to events inside Italy. Seeing the fate of these risings people began to link constitutionalism with independence, since it appeared that domestic freedom could prevail only as long as the Austrians did not suppress it. When the July revolution of 1830 brought a constitutional régime to power in France the conspirators hoped she would maintain a policy of international non-intervention and guard them against Austria.

Revolution broke out again in 1831, beginning in Modena and spreading rapidly to Parma, Bologna, the Marches and Umbria. Once again it lacked any widespread roots or any unifying cause. One group wanted to make Francesco IV of Modena – a fierce reactionary – into the head of a liberal national movement. He initially approved this plan but then changed his mind and had the plotters arrested on 3 February 1831, two days before their insurrection was due to begin. In Bologna resentment had been growing at the backwardness and restriction of clerical rule. The interlude between the death of Pope Pius VIII on 30 November 1830 and the election of Gregory XVI on 2 February 1831 allowed the plot to mature, and on 4 February 1831 a rising broke out in Bologna. Francesco IV promptly fled to Vienna for help, and the duchess of Parma took refuge with the Austrian garrison at Piacenza. In Bologna the aristocracy and higher bourgeoisie quickly seized the reins from the conspirators and set about dismantling papal government, issuing a constitution on 4 March 1831. At this point the revolution was undermined from outside. The future Napoleon III was plotting at Rome, and Metternich artfully put before king Louis-Philippe of France the spectre of Bonapartism established in central Italy. France at once recognized that Austrian intervention was a 'family affair' – the duke of Modena and the duchess of Parma were both members of the Austrian royal family – and Austrian troops moved in to crush the revolt, which ended on 26 March when the provisional government of Bologna capitulated.

Giuseppe Mazzini (1805–72) was born in Genoa, a hothouse of republicanism and nationalism, and grew up amidst the heated debate which raged there between revolutionaries and conservatives. He had joined a branch of the Carbonari in 1827 but soon became disillusioned by their lack of clear political purpose: 'My initiator had not uttered a syllable which gave a hint as to federalism or unity, as to republic or monarchy', he wrote later, 'just war against the government, no more.' He soon determined his own objective: to free Italy from Austrian occupation, indirect control by Vienna, princely despotism, aristocratic privilege and clerical authority. Arrested in November 1830, he was briefly imprisoned before being released and exiled the following January. It was whilst in prison that he developed the ideas which led him to found *Giovine Italia* (Young Italy) in 1832.

Mazzini's new patriotic revolutionary society was a reaction to the failure of 1820–1 and 1831, from which he concluded that the old revolutionaries had been too cautious and that the Italian nationalist movement had reached a point of maturity which put it ahead of its leadership. It was also a response to the widespread risings across Europe in 1830–2 which led many to feel that revolt was in the air. More specifically, Mazzini was influenced by a book published in 1831 by Buonarroti entitled *Reflections on Federal Government Applied to Italy*. In it the old revolutionary confessed to having abandoned his belief in a federal republic in favour of a unitary one as this was a better way to avoid social inequality and would be more able to defend itself. Buonarroti still believed, however, that before anything could happen in Italy there must be a democratic revolution in France. Mazzini scorned this 'wait and see' attitude, believing that Italy could make its own future.

Young Italy was founded, first, on a firm belief in progress, which had been stifled by the Restoration. Mazzini believed that God had given missions both to peoples and to nations, and the strong feelings of patriotic nationalism which he imparted to Young Italy were founded on his conviction that Italians could make themselves into a nation-state and that Italy had a mission in the free world. The second important characteristic of the movement was its emphasis on a united Italy, in contrast to the localism of other patriotic movements. Thirdly, Mazzini was a republican: only this form of government, he believed, could secure the equality of peoples.

Mazzini aimed to marry thought and action by the twin means of education and popular insurrection. In practical terms he was singularly unsuccessful. A plot hatched in Marseilles in 1833 to invade Savoy was denounced, and another, later in the same year, for a rising of patriots in Naples came to nothing. In February 1834, a small force of Mazzinians crossed the border from Switzerland into Savoy. When the local population failed to show any enthusiasm for the call to arms they at once retreated.

The fiasco of the invasion of Savoy ended the first phase of Mazzini's activities, and by February 1836 he reported that Young Italy had completely broken up. Mazzini himself fled to London in 1837 and remained there for the next eleven years. In 1839 he announced that he was going to reconstitute *Giovine Italia*, with the important addition of workers' groups: 'In the first period of our existence we worked for the People but not with the People'. However, he remained implacably hostile to socialism, believing that all classes must be united in the struggle for Italy and not divided against one another. And he ignored the agrarian problems which affected so deeply the everyday life of the peasant masses in many parts of Italy.

Mazzini's example spawned a succession of imitators. Risings in Sicily and the kingdom of Naples in 1837 and perpetual stirrings in the Papal States prompted Nicola Fabrizi to found the *Legione italica* (Italic Legion) in 1839 and try to link the various groups of plotters. An uprising in Naples planned for 31 July 1843 never took place and the bands which rose briefly and disorganizedly in the Papal States were soon crushed and their ringleaders executed. The Bandiera brothers, members of *Giovine Italia* who had founded their own secret society, tried to raise an insurrection in Calabria in June 1844. It failed and both brothers were taken and shot. Trouble was endemic throughout much of Italy on the eve of 1848, but it was of a local and narrowly based variety. Men were wooed by Mazzinian ideals; masses remained stubbornly uninterested in them.

In the years before 1848 most of Italy was economically backward. Apart from silk the main products were grain, oil, wine, wool, cotton and flax and these were chiefly produced for local consumption. External markets were hard to enter because of the high tariff walls which most states put up; and a marked tendency to put surplus profits into land, often for social reasons, deprived industry of much needed investment. Lombardy was the exception to this general picture. Here a favourable climate permitted the growth of mulberry trees, and silk became the dominant product. From 1824, as foreign markets expanded, Lombards sold initially to London and then, as first Indian and later Chinese and Japanese silk took over, they moved into French and German markets. Lombard silk producers chafed at the restrictive tariffs imposed on them by Vienna and were bitterly hostile to Austrian attempts to divert their trade from its traditional flow through Genoa and move it instead to Trieste, fearing that they would be stranded on the margin of European development.

If not directly interested in unification, Lombard businessmen became more interested in progress and economic development as they nurtured their export trade. The rules of the market place and developments in science and technology were of considerable importance to them, and newspapers and journals sprang up to give these economic liberals the knowledge they sought. It was in this area that connections could be made between freedom of trade and freedom of the individual. Writing in Florence's *Commercial Journal* on 14 July 1847, Camillo Cavour, a future prime minister of Italy, put the point clearly: 'We are convinced that in working to lower the barriers that divide us, we are working for the intellectual and moral progress of Italy as well as for its material prosperity.'

The tariff barriers put up by a divided Italy were a political obstacle to economic development. Another adverse consequence of political division was a poor communications network. Only Lombardy had a good road and canal network. The railway system was rudimentary; only three short stretches of railway existed in Austrian-controlled territory, together with one in

Piedmont and one in Naples. Régimes which were so backward dismayed and annoyed moderate liberals looking to improve their economic position and take advantage of the opportunities which a more modern state system of credit institutions, free trade and good communications could provide.

CULTURAL NATIONALISM

Alongside republican activists there existed by 1848 an influential group of moderates who propagated their ideas through books and journals. Cultural nationalism was first put forward in the review *Antologia (Anthology)*, founded in Florence in 1821 to spread literary ideas to a national audience. The other forerunner of the literary explosion of the 1840s was the journal *Universal Annals of Statistics, Public Economy, History, Travel and Commerce*, founded in Milan in 1824. The Congress of Italian Scientists, which first met at Pisa in 1839, was another expression of national consciousness as well as a vehicle for disseminating progressive ideas. Although political discussion was formally excluded, the debates on economic and social problems carried unmistakable undertones of reformism.

A spate of published histories made liberals much more aware of their national past. In 1839 Troya produced the first volume of his *History of Italy in the Middle Ages*. Nine years earlier, count Cesare Balbo had produced a *History of Italy under the Barbarians*, and he followed this with a *Summary of the History of Italy* in 1846. The Tuscan journal *Italian Historical Archive* and the Piedmontese Society for Patriotic History were part of the same phenomenon.

The first of a number of programmes for unification put forward during these years was Vincenzo Gioberti's *Of the Moral and Civil Primacy of the Italians*, published in 1843. A liberal catholic who believed that Mazzinian tactics had failed and who preferred to put his trust in princes, Gioberti believed that an Italian *risorgimento* would be the first step to the world hegemony of a reformed church. He proposed a confederation of states under the pope's leadership, supported by Piedmont: the union of Italy, he wrote, 'must commence where faith and force chiefly reside, that is, in the holy city and the warrior province'. Balbo's *Summary of the History of Italy* helped give a historical basis to the concept of the pope as the defender of Italian liberty.

An alternative prospectus for unification came when Balbo published *Of the Hopes of Italy* in 1844. Arguing that the Piedmontese monarchy was destined to lead Italy, he set the struggle firmly in a European frame. For Austria to be ousted from the peninsula would require assistance by the Great Powers. To Balbo, the immediate task was to build up a rational, moderate body of nationalist opinion. The argument for Piedmont as the natural leader of a united Italy was also put forcefully by Massimo d'Azeglio in *The Most Recent Events in Romagna* (1846) and *Proposal for a Programme for Italian National Opinion* (1847). D'Azeglio suggested that it was in the princes' interests to ally with the moderates who were seeking to liberate Italy from reaction: 'If Italian sovereigns do not want their subjects to become extreme liberals', he wrote, 'they must make themselves moderate liberals.' His programme included popularly elected communal councils, public trial by jury, progressive press laws, a general system of railways and the breaking down of internal commercial barriers.

Why had the revolts failed? Absolutist régimes had proved vulnerable to initial assault but had been able to recover with external assistance. This highlights the importance of the international alignment: until the Concert of Europe failed in 1824–5, Britain was prepared to support intervention by the Great Powers wherever order appeared threatened, and thereafter, as she retreated into domestic concerns, Austria remained able and willing to act as Europe's policeman. The revolutionaries had no mass support inside the states they sought to undermine, for the very good reason that they had not bothered to consider the need for it. Where moderates did achieve temporary success, their intense localism hindered the formation of any united front: in 1831 the provisional government of Bologna had been totally uninterested in helping the rebels in nearby Modena. Even within their own locales the uprisings had lacked the ability to galvanize support: artificial dynasticism, such as that underpinning the rising in Modena in 1831, and vague ideas of a constituent assembly were far too elusive, and even the Mazzinian slogans 'Republic', 'Progress' and 'Association' were abstruse and unintelligible to almost everybody. Before 1848 there existed in Italy neither a revolutionary situation in which generalized discontent could provide the tinder, nor a unifying ideology to keep the flames burning once a spark had lit the fire.

The first war of the Risorgimento, 1848-9

During 1847 the ingredients for revolution were created. Leadership of some kind was necessary to focus discontent, and the new pope, Pius IX, seemed to be prepared to provide it. His words and his deeds aroused the enthusiasm of those who struggled for liberal constitutional rule, those who fought for independence from Austria, and those who aspired to build a united Italy. Something akin to a revolutionary situation was also building up in consequence of the worsening economic plight of the masses. The catalyst was revolt in Sicily which caused the collapse of many absolutist rulers. They had been brought down before, but what now gave revolution its hour of success was the absence of foreign intervention. Austria was preoccupied with quelling revolutions of her own, and France was in the throes of unseating the conservative Orleanist monarchy and replacing it with the Second Republic. No other Great Power showed any interest in intervening. The struggles were again for independence and for liberty – but were they for Italy?

THE COMING OF REVOLUTION

In June 1846 Pius IX became pope. His liberal reputation was confirmed when he amnestied many political prisoners, set up commissions to study reform of the civil and criminal law procedures and announced a railway programme. These moves generated pressure for further political reforms such as freedom of the press and the formation of a civic guard. Fears that a clericalist conspiracy was about to seize the pope and massacre the liberals led to the formation of such a guard in July 1847; and in the same month the Austrians, alarmed by what was happening in Rome,

10

occupied Ferrara and threatened to move into the Papal Legations, evoking a general wave of patriotic protest throughout Italy.

During the autumn of 1847 a third force was added to those of reformism and patriotism. After two disastrous years the harvest was better, but prices stayed high and Italy was now hit by the effects of the European economic crisis. Everywhere in the countryside, but particularly in Sicily, peasants who depended heavily on common rights of grazing, gathering wood or berries and hunting, tried to recover lands which had been illegally enclosed since 1815. An undercurrent of more or less continuous peasant agitation lasted into 1848, adding to the instability of the absolutist princes.

During the same period repression and concession marched hand in hand in Italy. Riots in Milan and Reggio Calabria were suppressed, but minor reforms in Tuscany and Piedmont whetted appetites for further change. The different struggles were coming to be linked in the popular mind: on 8 November, when Milan celebrated the appointment of an Italian, Carlo Bartolomeo Romilli, as archbishop in succession to an Austrian, the streets rang with cries of 'Viva Pio IX, viva l'Italia'. The police cracked down on the demonstration, killing one and wounding sixty. At the end of December 1847 a new ministry was announced in Rome composed entirely of cardinals, disappointing those who were expecting a lay government. A major demonstration occurred on 1 January 1848, and public alarm increased with the news that the Austrians had moved into Parma and Modena. In Tuscany and at Genoa moderate democrats agitated for a civic guard to protect and further their rights.

As part of a mounting anti-Austrian campaign in Lombardy, professor Giovanni Cantori invited the citizens of Milan to give up smoking – tobacco was a government monopoly – from 1 January 1848. The gesture brought a huge response. The viceroy retaliated by ordering out police with cigars to provoke the crowd and then arrest trouble-makers. The Austrian army joined in, and on 3 January six demonstrators were killed and fifty wounded. Trouble was flaring up and down the peninsula, connected by reformism and anti-Austrian patriotism but essentially responding to local situations and developments. One major act of general significance could turn the local fires into a general conflagration. It came far away to the south, in Sicily.

On 9 January 1848 a manifesto appeared on the streets of Palermo urging Sicilians to take arms to recover their legitimate rights. Behind these bold words was no real organization, merely agreement between a small number of patriots to go onto the streets and raise the people. After a hesitant beginning on 12 January, the insurgency gathered pace as Sicilians of all classes massed in a campaign to regain their constitution of 1812 and throw off Bourbon mainland rule. On 2 February the general committee at Palermo assumed the powers of a provisional government and by the middle of the month the only Bourbon troops left on the island were locked up at Syracuse and Messina.

Insurrection spread to the mainland on 17 January and Ferdinand II quickly collapsed before the spectre of revolution. His chief of police and his confessor were both exiled, a new ministry was formed and on 29 January a royal decree announced the introduction of a constitution. Although it included provision for an elected chamber, real power remained in the crown's hands. The decree was joyfully accepted in Naples and disdainfully rejected by Palermo. However, the wall of absolutism had been breached at last. On 8 February Charles Albert, king of Piedmont, gave way to pressure and published a draft constitution, which guaranteed press freedom and freedom of association but kept most powers in the hands of the crown. On 15 February Tuscany followed suit.

By March 1848 compromises between absolutist monarchs and moderates had calmed the agitation almost everywhere. But Palermo fought on for autonomy, and in Lombardy–Venetia some 70,000 Austrian troops were massed to hold down riots and to intervene elsewhere in Italy. The news of the fall of Metternich on 14 March and the introduction of the Austrian constitution two days later was the signal for northern Italy to try to shake off Austrian domination.

CATTANEO AND MILAN

When the news of Metternich's fall reached Milan on 17 March, moderates who wanted concessions from Austria temporarily

12

joined forces with radicals who wanted insurrection. The key figure in this alliance was Carlo Cattaneo (1801–69). A lawyer who had made a close study of economics, Cattaneo was a liberal republican but not a democrat. He was also a federalist, distrusting Piedmont as a potential instrument of oppression and looking to an Italian congress to be held in Rome to decide Italy's future. Above all he was a municipalist, concerned with the defence of political liberty in his own region rather than with Italian independence.

Fighting against the Austrian troops began in Milan on 18 March, and moderates led by the mayor, Gabriele Casati, appealed to Piedmont for help 'to chase the common enemy beyond the Alps'. This was moving in a direction which seemed dangerous to Cattaneo, who was excluded from the provisional government then formed. After 'the glorious five days', Milan drove out the Austrian commander Radetzky who retired to Verona, one of only two cities in Lombardy–Venetia which had not rid themselves of the occupier. Cattaneo then threw in his lot with the moderates and agreed to defer discussions about the form of future government *a guerra vinta* (until the war is won). A victory for the moderates, this represented the triumph of local municipal loyalty over all else.

The Milanese request for help reached Turin on the evening of 23 March and next day Charles Albert announced his intention to aid Lombardy against the Austrians, harping on the theme of national liberation and putting his faith in 'that God who has put Italy in a position to be able to act by herself'. The king of Piedmont saw the chance to add Lombardy to his possessions; he also wanted to support the moderates and prevent the victory of Milanese republicanism, which would threaten his own régime and possibly encourage Great Power intervention.

Cattaneo, who feared that Milanese republicanism would be suffocated if Piedmont took over the crusade against Austria, worked to prevent the Lombard army being put under Piedmontese control. He then tried to break the moderate government, summon a Lombard assembly and ask France to intervene. Mazzini, who had arrived in Milan, undermined him by emphasizing the need to gain independence first, whereas Cattaneo saw

13

the first requisites as the establishment of a republic and democracy. The results of a plebiscite called by Charles Albert, which were published on 8 June, confirmed Cattaneo's defeat. Invited to vote for or against fusion with Piedmont, 561,002 cast their votes for annexation and only 681 for delay. Within two months, Cattaneo's suspicions about Charles Albert were to be borne out.

CHARLES ALBERT'S WAR

National war was a military humiliation. The Piedmontese army, totally unprepared for an offensive campaign, moved slowly across Lombardy towards Verona where Radetzky was awaiting reinforcements from Vienna, and failed to prevent the arrival of an Austrian relief force. June was spent in inactivity as Charles Albert awaited the results of the Lombard plebiscite. He was now prepared to settle for Lombardy and the duchies of Parma and Modena, but was under pressure from the forces he had set himself to head. His own government would accept no solution which was not based on Austrian troops evacuating Italy.

On 25 July Radetzky's armies overwhelmed the Piedmontese at the battle of Custozza. Charles Albert retreated, aware that he could only begin to negotiate with Vienna when his troops were out of Lombardy. The problem was Milan, still a seedbed of republicanism: if it continued fighting, whether successfully or not, the example of its heroism would stand in glaring contrast to the failure of the regular army and give a new lease of life to republicanism. The king solved the difficulty by retreating to the city and then handing it over to the Austrians. Charles Albert announced the armistice with Austria on 10 August, adding 'the cause of Italian independence is not yet lost'.

In the months that followed, international events turned against Italy. The Emperor Ferdinand's military commander, Prince Windischgrätz, subdued a revolt in Vienna by 1 November, and attempts at international mediation between Vienna and Turin collapsed when it became clear that France would not intervene to help Piedmont. By November the Great Powers had decided that Italy should revert to the borders of 1815. However, the internal forces which were unleashed by the revolt were not willing to comply. Democrats took power in Piedmont in December, prepared to continue the war rather than surrender to Austria. Charles Albert was happy to fall in with these ideas: he wanted to restore the lost prestige of the monarchy and to re-enter Milan as liberator, and the democrats were prepared to offer him command of the army – a necessary political move, but militarily unwise.

The second round of war began on 20 March 1849 and ended three days later with the defeat of the Piedmontese at the battle of Novara. Charles Albert abdicated that night in favour of his eldest son, Victor Emmanuel, and left at once for Spain – so hurriedly that he forgot to sign a formal act of abdication. Victor Emmanuel met Radetzky at Vignale on the afternoon of 24 March 1849 to discuss peace terms. A legend later grew up that at that meeting the new king refused the offer of an expansion of the kingdom in exchange for abolishing the constitution and giving up the red, white and green tricolour. In fact Radetzky never proposed the abolition of the constitution, but offered Victor Emmanuel an easier peace if he was prepared to turn against the democrats. This the new king was willing to do, making it abundantly clear that he approved neither of the democrats nor of the resumption of the war and that he proposed to rule in an authoritiarian manner. This was eminently acceptable to Austria, and the armistice was agreed on 26 March.

MANIN AND THE VENETIAN REPUBLIC

In January 1848 Daniele Manin (1804–57), the leading Venetian politician, petitioned that Lombardy and Venetia be 'truly national and Italian', calling for Vienna to relinquish control of the army and navy and of finances, and for the abolition of tithes and the introduction of freedom of speech. For this the Austrian authorities threw him into prison, from which he was released by a popular revolt on 17 March after news of Metternich's fall had reached Venice. Five days later news of the uprising in Milan prompted Manin to lead a revolt which quickly toppled the Austrians. For the next eighteen months Manin was the dominant figure as Venice first manoeuvred and then fought for its independence.

Although conscious of an Italian national feeling, Manin was first and foremost a municipalist, like Cattaneo, and fought for his city. Secondly, and no less powerfully, he was a bourgeois republican with no socialist ideals. He pursued enlightened policies – controlling the price of bread, raising wages and guaranteeing the jobs of municipal workers. Like Cattaneo, he too agreed to postpone any decision on the form of government of an independent Venice *a guerra finita*.

When, on 8 June, the province of Venetia voted overwhelmingly for fusion with Lombardy in a new constitutional kingdom, Venice was left to continue the crusade against Austria alone. A period of confusion followed in which some argued for fusion, others for sticking to the agreed policy of postponing decisions, and yet others for appealing to the French Republic for help. Manin was chary of Charles Albert, fearing that he would sell out Venetia to the Austrians in return for Lombardy – which he was indeed prepared to do. Then, on 23 June, the suppression of the workers' insurrection in Paris ended any hope of French intervention to help a fellow republic. Needing Piedmontese troops to maintain Venice's independence, Manin allowed himself to be persuaded to accept fusion on 3 July. Three weeks later Charles Albert's army crashed to defeat at Custozza.

Isolated and chronically short of money – other Italian states would not buy Venetian bonds or accept Venetian paper money – Venice was not yet quite alone. Piedmont tried a second time to defeat Austria by force of arms and in March 1849 the newly formed Roman republic approached Venice with a view to forming a democratic bloc. Manin was forced to reject this because he needed Piedmontese military support, but Charles Albert failed him at the battle of Novara.

After Novara Venice decided to fight on. Manin's hopes that Britain and France might yet intervene to save the infant republic were in vain: the Second Republic showed no wish to undertake risky foreign ventures, and Palmerston said on 20 April 1849 that the time had come for peace at any price. In a last diplomatic throw Venice allied herself with Hungary on 20 May 1849. Finally alone after the collapse of the Roman republic, short of food and ammunition, bombarded by Austrian artillery and gripped by cholera, the city received news of the collapse of the Hungarian revolution on 19 August 1849. Negotiations were opened at once and eight days later Austrian troops entered the Piazza San Marco. Manin left for exile the following day.

THE ROMAN REPUBLIC

Pius IX tried during the early months of 1848 to calm popular agitation and reinforce papal authority, although by asking God's blessing for Italy he excited patriots. A constitution was granted on 13 March and fifteen days later, after hearing news of risings in Vienna and Milan, Pius acceded to a request from Piedmont and agreed to station troops on the frontier with Venetia to keep the Austrians occupied. Pushed by the lay majority in the government, the Pope allowed his troops to cross the river Po on 21 April. Immediately Austria made its hostility known, and faced with the possibility of a schism in the Catholic Church Pius IX withdrew from the national struggle, announcing on 29 April that he had no temporal ambitions. Contemporaries regarded this as an act of betrayal; historians have tended to see it as the collapse of an artificially created myth of a liberal pope.

By September the situation in the Papal States was tense. In an attempt to recover lost ground the Pope installed Pellegrino Rossi as head of an administration on 16 September 1848. Rossi inaugurated a programme of public order and his measures, which included decreasing the freedom of the press and expanding the powers of the police, aroused the anger of democrats. When parliament was opened on 15 November Rossi was murdered. Nine days later the Pope fled to Gaeta to take refuge with the king of Naples. The Roman deputies handed power to a three-man Junta, backed by a massive democratic movement in the provinces, and patriots flooded into Rome, among them Giuseppe Garibaldi. The Junta announced at the end of December that it was calling an assembly to be elected by direct universal suffrage. The assembly met on 5 February 1849 and five days later it declared Rome a republic.

Forces began to mass against the infant republic from the moment of its birth. On 8 February came news that Austrian

17

troops had reoccupied Ferrara, and Bourbon troops were known to be gathering in the south. When the news arrived of Piedmont's defeat at Novara on 23 March power was handed over to a triumvirate which included Mazzini. Rome was now in a hopeless position: Austria and France were both determined to restore the Pope, and no other Great Power opposed them. French troops landed at Civitavecchia on 24 April and marched on Rome, attacking the city six days later. During May the Austrians advanced into the Papal States, taking Bologna, Ancona and Perugia; the republic was attacked by Ferdinand II; and 4000 Spaniards landed and took Terracina, on the border with the kingdom of Naples. On 4 June 35,000 French troops launched their big assault. After a month of hard fighting the city decided to receive them 'impassively' on 2 July. That night Garibaldi left the city to carry on the fight. After a tortuous journey, during which his wife Anita died, he reached Genoa the following year and then left for Liverpool and New York. He did not return to Italy for four years. Mazzini meanwhile had slipped out of Civitavecchia on 12 July in disguise and using an American passport.

NAPLES AND SICILY

Sicilian rebels, unwilling to accept Ferdinand II's concession of an island parliament, were encouraged by the rising in Milan. A provisional government declared on 13 April 1848 that Ferdinand and his successors were forever banned from the throne of Sicily and announced that once the constitution had been reformed an Italian prince would be called to the throne. This measure was designed to guarantee necessary British support and to mollify those who feared that the new régime might drift too far towards the revolutionaries who wanted to bring about social change.

On the mainland, news of Milan's 'five days' produced anti-Austrian riots (see p. 13). A core of artisans and workers in Naples began to spread revolutionary ideas but the *lazzari* (the masses of Neapolitan poor) remained loyal to Ferdinand II. Clashes between the crown and the moderate government in April and May ended when Ferdinand II dissolved the assembly and the Naples national guard on 17 May. The mainland democrats made no attempt to ally with the peasants who were agitating almost everywhere, and by mid-July their risings had been crushed. On 7 September the reactionary Raffaele Longobardi took over the ministry of the interior and absolutism was restored to the mainland.

Separatism in Sicily looked as if it would be the midwife of democracy. In July, after four months' labour, an elected parliament produced a constitution which was by contemporary standards very advanced since it contained the principle of popular sovereignty. The king then offered the island its own parliament, army and administration but this was emphatically rejected. Then, on 28 February 1849, in the so-called Act of Gaeta, Ferdinand made his final offer. Sicily would be ruled by a viceroy but would have its own parliament, separate finances, Sicilian ministers and Sicilian public employees. To accept meant capitulation, to reject meant war without British or French support. The island prevaricated – and moderates changed sides as the gangs which had been used to oust the Bourbons got out of control and socialist demands for land nationalization were put forward. On 19 March 1849 Ferdinand announced that the truce was over and ten days later general Carlo Filangieri began the process of recapturing the island. Cities fell one by one and finally, on 15 April 1849, Palermo was back in Bourbon hands.

Why did the revolution of 1848–9 fail? The first and most obvious answer is that the power vacuum left by Austria's withdrawal was only temporary. Once Vienna had regained domestic control it was free to crush the Italian revolts. They in turn could find no outside support; only France seemed likely to sympathize with republican revolutionaries, but Louis-Napoleon Bonaparte was more concerned to reassure French Catholics of his moderacy by restoring the Pope than to assist the young plant of nationalism. Secondly, the various revolts had been at heart localist not nationalist; a symbol of this was the flag of the Venetian republic, the red, white and green Italian tricolour with the lion of St Mark in one corner. Charles Albert had fought for Piedmont, Cattaneo for Milan, Manin for Venice, Romans for their republic and Sicilians for their island. In 1848 no one fought for Italy. Thirdly, the revolutionaries were still politically divided; the suspension of debate about the nature of government in Milan and Venice *a guerra vinta* is evidence of this.

The failure of 1848 was of great importance in the history of the Risorgimento, for it helped to clarify certain facts. Insurrection would not work. Any attempt at progress required united effort if it was to stand a chance of success. Such an effort would fail without a committed leadership which all could accept. And any common political programme must not antagonize those prepared to fight for independence; middle-class nationalists did not want socialism at any price. Also foreign support was vital if Austrian rule was to end. The diversity of ideas and aims had divided patriots. Failure awoke acknowledgement of the need to find a common denominator. But until the question 'What *kind* of Italy?' could be answered with some degree of unanimity, the unification of Italy remained a dream.

What kind of Italy? Mazzini and Cavour, 1849–59

FIRST REACTIONS TO 1848

Austrian rule was quickly restored and extended in northern Italy. In Lombardy–Venetia Radetzky instituted a policy of harsh repression, which alienated the masses, and raised the land tax by one-third, angering property owners. Austrian troops occupied Tuscany until 1855 and the Papal Legations until 1859; and Vienna also propped up the duchies of Parma and Modena. Links were tightened by a trade treaty between Austria and Lombardy in 1851 and by a five-year customs union between Austria, Parma and Modena in 1852. In the kingdom of the Two Sicilies the constitutional régime ended in March 1849 when the chamber was dissolved. Gestures were made to Sicilian separatism by creating a separate administration and a minister for Sicily, but the island was ruled by a lieutenant governor and the king of Naples had ultimate authority. Under this despotic rule the peasantry fared badly and the nobility well: the hated *macinato* (grain tax) was reintroduced and raised, but the land tax was kept at 1 per cent and the nobility profited from the sale of land previously held in common and thus extended their holdings.

The autopsy on 1848 now began, and with it came the demise of Mazzinian republicanism. The challenge was mounted first by Giuseppe Ferrari in *Philosophy and Revolution*, published in 1851. Ferrari believed aid from France was essential if an Italian revolution were to succeed, and rejected Mazzini's outdated belief in political revolution alone, arguing that Italy must also have a social revolution. Mazzini responded by publishing a manifesto which contained the vague outlines of a socio-economic programme, and began once more to build up conspiratorial groups in the Papal States, Tuscany and Lombardy. At this stage republicans and socialists shared the view that an Italian national revolution could only come about as part of a larger European revolution and looked to the French Second Republic to rekindle the fires of 1848. Their hopes were dashed when Louis-Napoleon Bonaparte's coup d'état of 2 December 1851 ended the life of the Second Republic.

In Piedmont–Sardinia elections in December 1849 produced a chamber dominated by conservatives. Pressure from the king and from among the Right to suspend the *Statuto* of March 1848 could have killed off Piedmontese Liberalism at this point but the premier, Massimo d'Azeglio, successfully resisted it. A second danger was that Piedmontese political development might be frozen into the conservative monarchical constitutionalism which the *Statuto* represented – *nulla di più, null di meno* (no more, no less). What prevented this was pressure to reform ecclesiastical legislation and end clerical privileges such as independent jurisdiction. The separation of Turin from the Papacy which now began was an important step in creating a new focus for patriotic feelings. The Church had betrayed national revolution and constitutional government: supporting Piedmont struck a blow against it as well as a blow for Italy.

MAZZINI AND PISACANE: THE FAILURE OF INSURRECTION

In April 1853 Mazzini rechristened his party the Party of Action and altered its membership to increase working-class representation. His tactics also changed: acknowledging that the towns were too well policed he determined to raise the rural masses by the example of small bands of patriots. Four attempts to raise the people of Lunigiana between September 1853 and July 1856 failed utterly, and as a consequence Mazzini began to feel for an alliance with the socialists. They were prepared to enter into a working relationship with him since their hopes of outside help from France had been dashed with the coup d'état of December 1851. The new grouping was justified by the theory of the *bandiera neutra* (neutral flag): ideological debates would be suspended in order to unite differing political elements for a common programme of action. As a consequence of this shift in policy Mazzini formed an accord with an intelligent if somewhat wayward soldier, Carlo Pisacane.

Carlo Pisacane (1818–57) had served in the army of the king of Naples before appearing in London in 1847. There he met and mingled with republican and socialist exiles before returning in 1848 to fight first for Piedmont and then for the Roman republic. Pisacane was a socialist with well-developed ideas about class interests and the dangers of collaborating with the middle classes. He did not believe that the interests of proletariat and bourgeoisie could be brought into political accord and had no great respect for Mazzinian insurrectionists, criticizing particularly their lack of a social programme: 'A people which rises before it knows what remedies to apply to its ills is lost', he wrote.

Two things moved Pisacane to action. He was alarmed at the consequences of Piedmont's participation in the Crimean war (1854–6), which seemed likely to gain her acknowledgement as the force best capable of unifying Italy, since he bitterly opposed Cavour's policies; and he believed that the anti-bourgeois forces had a chance of victory because social and political repression had reached insupportable levels, while conservative and anti-popular elements were not yet cohesive enough to hold down any revolt. This seemed particularly true of the south, and two small uprisings in Sicily in November 1856 encouraged the Party of Action to look there for success.

Pisacane landed at Sapri on 28 June 1857 with a force of some 350 men. All the signs were bad: the local organization was unready; the authorities had been alerted; local leaders had decided not to act until there were clear signs that the venture would be successful; and most of the peasants were away in Apulia working on the harvest. Insurrections at Livorno and Genoa, planned by Mazzini to spur the locals, failed to come off. Expecting to be swollen with large numbers of enthusiastic peasants, the band was joined by a single old man. On 1 July it fought an action against local forces in which some 150 of Pisacane's followers were killed. The survivors were cornered the following day after the inhabitants of a nearby village had turned on them, and Pisacane was killed. His death went to prove that the masses were quite unready to throw in their lot with revolutionaries whose aims they neither understood nor sympathized with.

CAVOUR AND THE FOUNDATION OF PIEDMONT'S PREDOMINANCE

Count Camillo Benso di Cavour (1810–61) was born in Turin, the second son of a conservative aristocrat. After four years' service in the army he resigned his commission in 1831 and travelled widely in Europe, visiting France, England, Switzerland and Belgium. He became an expert on agricultural and commercial development. He also witnessed the July revolution and this made him a lifelong opponent of republicanism and socialism, as well as of the anti-rationalism of conservative dynasties. His political path was soon determined; he wrote to a friend in March 1833, 'I can tell you that I am genuinely for the *juste milieu*, desiring, wishing, working for social progress with all my powers, but determined not to buy it at the price of a general political and social upheaval.' To hold off anarchy on one side and despotism on the other, Cavour developed a system based on the leadership of a rational élite buttressed by a parliament elected by the educated and responsible minority. Such ideas made Guizot in France and Peel in Britain Conservatives. In Piedmont, they made Cavour a Liberal.

Cavour entered the Piedmontese government in October 1850 as minister for agriculture, becoming premier for the first time twenty-five months later. The basis of his dominance of Piedmontese politics, which he maintained until his death, lay in the joint resistance he engineered in February 1852 between the two major political groupings in the Piedmontese parliament – his own centre-right party and Ratazzi's centre-left group – against the king's desire to introduce trial without jury for press offences. The *connubio* (marriage), as this was called, gave Cavour considerable freedom for manoeuvre. A broad body of support in the middle of the political spectrum enabled him to hold at bay the extremes of Mazzinian republicanism and monarchic dictatorship; it also permitted him to shift his political ground according to circumstances, manoeuvring to the right if he wished to muzzle the press, or to the left if he wished to stimulate nationalist feeling; and it provided him with a basis of parliamentary support over a long period of time. However, Cavour has been charged with leaving behind a bitter legacy. To some he is the father of *transformismo*, the practice of remaking cabinets in order to include dissenting elements and to evade dangerous parliamentary criticism which figured large in Liberal Italy and against which Fascism was a reaction. Also the *connubio* blocked the growth of a multi-party system; in its place, Italian politics came to revolve around single monolithic leaders – Cavour, Depretis, Crispi and ultimately Mussolini.

Cavour built up solid economic foundations on which to base Piedmont's expansion. He broke down protectionism by concluding bi-lateral treaties with France, Britain, Belgium and Austria. Under his general guidance new techniques were introduced in agriculture; iron works, foundries and factories expanded; the merchant fleet increased; the *Banca Nazionale* was founded; and railways, roads and telegraphs were all extended. The position of the Church was also weakened as ecclesiastical tribunals and rights of asylum were abolished and civil marriage introduced. In 1855 Cavour challenged the king and the old Right by passing a law suppressing all convents not dedicated to preaching, teaching or caring for the sick. These anti-clerical policies began to alienate the Papacy and in consequence attracted moderate democrats and wavering republicans.

In 1852 Cavour met Napoleon III. He quickly realized that Piedmontese expansion must have outside support, the missing factor in 1848; to a fellow nationalist, Michelangelo Castelli, he

24

wrote on 7 September 1852, 'our destiny depends above all on France. Whether we like it or not we shall have to be her partner in the great contest which must be played out sooner or later in Europe.' The opportunity came in 1854. Later, historians of the Risorgimento portrayed Piedmontese involvement in the Crimean War as the calculated act of a far-seeing statesman who planned to gain Great Power sympathy as the first stage in a programme of expansion. The truth was rather different. Cavour himself wanted only to lever very minor concessions out of Vienna, but Victor Emmanuel II was eager to enter the war – and even offered to command the allied armies. On 9 January 1855 the premier learned from the French representative at Turin that the king intended to oust him, bring in a conservative chief minister and join the war. Sooner than see the crown circumvent parliament and impose a ministry upon it, which would undercut the progress parliament had made since 1852, Cavour preferred to accede to war.

At the Congress of Paris which followed the conclusion of hostilities Cavour tried to use international sympathy to weaken Austrian domination of north Italy. His scheme to unseat the Habsburg rulers of the duchies of Parma and Modena failed when Britain refused to break up the Turkish empire in order to find a Danubian principality for one of the dukes. This forced Cavour to acknowledge that diplomatic manoeuvre alone would not advance the Piedmontese cause, and that there was 'only one truly effective solution to the Italian question: cannon'.

Cavour needed international sympathy to act against Austria, and Piedmont's constitutional government was one factor which secured it. He also needed to woo Italian patriots away from republicanism and socialism. Giorgio Pallavicino, founder of the Italian National Society, played a key role in this. From 1851 Pallavicino worked tirelessly to convert those who had taken part in 1848 to the cause of Piedmont, arguing that to want independence was to want the means of gaining it and that the only available means was the Piedmontese army. That and national opinion were, in his view, the two 'living forces of Italy' and he set out to link them up. This meant persuading patriots of many hues to sink their differences until Austria was ejected from the peninsula: 'First independence,

25

then liberty'. He attracted first Manin, then Cattaneo, and finally Giuseppe Garibaldi, the charismatic partisan general whose bands had performed rather better than the regular army. Cavour encouraged the Society, formally founded in 1857, to publicize its aims and to organize the volunteers who began to swarm into Piedmont, realizing that it attracted to his following the many democrats who disagreed with Mazzini's techniques.

Piedmontese armies and enthusiastic volunteers would not suffice to throw the Austrians out of north Italy. To succeed, the new Italian nationalism needed active French support. Paradoxically, an attempt by an Italian *carbonaro*, Felice Orsini, to assassinate Napoleon III on 14 January 1858 provided the impetus to bring Paris to support Turin. At his trial Orsini made an impassioned plea to the French emperor to make Italy independent, saying that there would be no peace in Europe until he did so. Napoleon was impressed, and in May 1858 made secret overtures to Cavour. He offered an alliance against Austria in return for a marriage between his nephew and Victor Emmanuel's daughter. At a secret meeting at Plombières on 20 July – about which Cavour did not consult his cabinet – the deal was struck. It reveals very clearly Cavour's limited aims. After provoking a war with Austria, Napoleon proposed dividing Italy into four: a kingdom of Upper Italy, to include Piedmont–Sardinia, Lombardy, Venetia and the Romagna; Rome and its surrounds, to be ruled by the Pope; a separate kingdom of Central Italy carved from the remainder of the Papal States and Tuscany; and a southern kingdom about which nothing was said. In exchange for helping to bring this about Napoleon asked for the Piedmontese marriage and for Nice and Savoy. The treaty of alliance was signed on 26 January 1859 and the wedding took place four days later.

At the last moment Cavour's careful manoeuvring seemed to be about to come to nought. Not only did the British offer to mediate between Piedmont and Austria, but France appeared to be having second thoughts. Then, on 23 April 1859, an Austrian ultimatum was handed over in Turin demanding that the Piedmontese army be put back on a peacetime footing and that the regiments of volunteers formed under the aegis of the Italian National Society be disbanded. Cavour rejected the demand, and war broke out on 29 April.

The triumph of Piedmont, 1859–70

All Cavour's diplomatic skill and his appetite for expansion would have counted for little had he not been favoured with a benign international environment when Piedmont launched out on what became the conquest of Italy. Russia, still smarting from Austria's failure to support her during the Crimean war, agreed not to intervene in Italy on her behalf; and Prussia, humiliated by Austria at Olmütz nine years earlier when she had sought a share in the control of Germany, was no better disposed towards Vienna. France was prepared to see an expanded Piedmont in northern Italy as a check on Austria. And Britain was now willing to give Piedmontese ambitions active support.

The Italian cause was a popular one in Britain. There was great admiration for Italian culture; Piedmont's anti-clerical legislation appealed to anti-papal feelings; Sicilian sulphur mines and Italian railways offered the opportunity for investment and profit; Garibaldi was hero-worshipped by the working classes and high society alike; and the king of Naples was detested. Queen Victoria expressed a deeply held feeling when she wrote that 'as a Liberal constitutional country, opposing a barrier alike to unenlightened and absolute as well as revolutionary principles . . . she [Piedmont] has a right to expect us to support her'. Finally, the general election of 1859 had placed at the helm of British politics a prime minister, Palmerston, who was anti-Austrian and who calculated that backing Piedmont would reduce French power on the continent. Circumstances favoured Piedmont in 1859, and they continued to do so until the moment when Rome was finally gained eleven years later.

THE WAR OF 1859 AND THE ANNEXATION OF CENTRAL ITALY

Victor Emmanuel commanded a combined army of 93,000 Italians and 200,000 French for only eighteen days, during which time the Austrian army made no significant moves, before Napoleon III arrived to take supreme command on 14 May. The combined forces moved towards Milan, and French troops fought a bloody battle at Magenta on 4 June, after which the Austrians abandoned Milan and pulled back east. Garibaldi's partisans meanwhile captured Brescia and Salò in the north. Franz Josef now took personal command of the Austrian forces and moved his army forward to meet the advancing allied troops. On 24 June the Austrians were defeated in simultaneous battles against the French at Solferino and the Piedmontese at San Martino.

The war had meanwhile stimulated a chain of uprisings which were to present Cavour with a severe dilemma. A Tuscan insurrection on 27 April ejected the grand-duke and made Victor Emmanuel II protector of the province for the duration of the war. The rulers of Parma and Modena decamped after the battle of Magenta and the duchies sought annexation by Turin. Austrian troops were recalled from Bologna at the same time, and the population offered Victor Emmanuel 'dictatorship'. Popular disturbance quickly spread southwards through the Papal Legations and into Umbria and the Marches.

Nationalism was spreading faster than Napoleon III had expected. To continue the war would be to suffer more heavy casualties. It would also put central Italy into Piedmont's hands. Sooner than do this, Napoleon III unilaterally proposed an armistice on 5 July and Franz Josef accepted three days later. The terms hammered out by the two emperors gave most of Lombardy to France, who would pass it on to Turin; Venetia remained part of the Austrian empire; the rulers of Tuscany and Modena were to be returned to their thrones; and papal government was to be restored to the Legations. Cavour wanted to dissuade Victor Emmanuel from accepting these terms and resigned when the king refused to follow his line. Since Venetia had not been handed over in accordance with the Pact of Plombières, Nice and Savoy remained in Piedmontese hands.

Popular feeling now moved to Piedmont's aid. A representative assembly elected in Tuscany on 7 August unanimously proclaimed the previous dynasty fallen for ever and thirteen days later voted to become part of the constitutional kingdom of Victor Emmanuel. Parma, Modena and the Papal Legations expressed the same popular mood. While the four central states formed military and customs unions, Piedmontese diplomats attending the peace

28

conference in Zurich successfully resisted the idea that a regent be appointed to rule over all four together.

In January 1860 Cavour returned to power convinced that France could be persuaded to accept Piedmont's annexation of the four central Italian states in return for Savoy and Nice. When Napoleon III countered with the idea of an independent Tuscany, which would be a block to unification, the premier decided to recruit democracy to back his diplomacy. Plebiscites based on universal suffrage were held in Tuscany and Emilia in March 1860 in which voters were offered the choice between 'annexation to the constitutional monarchy of king Victor Emmanuel II' or a 'separate kingdom' of no specified kind. In Emilia 427,512 voted out of an electorate of 526,218 (81 per cent), of whom 426,006 chose annexation; in Tuscany 386,445 out of 534,000 voted (73 per cent), with 366,571 in favour of annexation. Both states were declared integral parts of the Piedmontese–Sardinian kingdom by royal decree, and on 1 April 1860 it was announced that Savoy and Nice would be ceded to France in exchange. Here democracy worked retrospectively: plebiscites held on 15 and 22 April produced overwhelming majorities for union with France – 85 per cent in Nice and 97 per cent in Savoy.

GARIBALDI AND SICILY

On the night of 3/4 April 1860 a master plumber named Francisco Riso started a small insurrection in Palermo. It was quickly put down and thirteen of the ringleaders were shot. This retaliation by the Bourbon authorities rapidly produced an unexpectedly dramatic reaction: riots broke out in other cities across the island and soon armed gangs controlled the countryside, as they had done in 1848. The revolutionary situation for which southern republicans had been hoping suddenly seemed to be developing. The movement lacked only a leader and a leading Sicilian republican, Francesco Crispi, asked Garibaldi to take up the banner of independence.

Garibaldi was under pressure to go to Nice, the city of his birth, and lead a campaign against the plebiscite there. But he was persuaded to go south after Crispi showed him a telegram – probably forged – saying that revolution was surging through the Sicilian countryside. Cavour was deeply concerned about the international consequences if Garibaldi went to Sicily, to Nice or into the Papal States as he appeared to be contemplating, as any one of these acts might well provoke Great Power intervention and lose Piedmont the goodwill she enjoyed. He failed to stop the expedition but did prevent the king from giving it his open support.

Garibaldi landed at Marsala on 10 May 1860, accompanied by his famous *Mille* (Thousand) – actually 1088 men and 1 woman. Half of his force was of bourgeois origin and the other half was made up of artisans and workers. The largest single group came from Lombardy, and there were only forty-five Sicilians in the party. As his band confronted 25,000 Bourbon troops who were occupying the island his chances of success appeared slight. Whatever the outcome, Cavour hoped to profit from it: writing six days after the landing, he stated, 'If the Sicilian insurrection is crushed we shall say nothing; if it succeeds we shall intervene in the name of humanity and order'. He hoped either to rid himself of a patriot who was also a democrat with republican sympathies or to scoop his embarrassing ally's success.

Two forces came to Garibaldi's aid and allowed him to achieve the impossible. One was the traditional separatism of the Sicilian middle and upper classes. Bourbon attempts to conciliate these groups after the revolutions of 1820–1 by abandoning stamp and tobacco duties and by not reintroducing conscription failed to woo them to Naples, largely because the mainland government insisted on trying to press ahead with land reform. This action also gave birth to the second element which destabilized Sicily: peasant unrest. With the legal ending of feudalism big landlords carried out a ruthless policy of enclosing common lands. The peasantry lost a battery of rights upon which they depended to live: to cut wood, to collect acorns and chestnuts, to burn limestone, to glean stubble and most importantly to pasture animals. The slow and incomprehensible processes of the law helped them not one whit.

On 13 May Garibaldi announced that he was assuming the dictatorship of Sicily in the name of Victor Emmanuel II, and two days later he won an important victory against Bourbon troops at

Calatafimi. He then attacked Palermo and after failing to get any clear instructions from Naples its commander surrendered to him on 6 June. Garibaldi now divided the island into twenty-four districts, each with a governor, ended many of the Bourbon taxes and duties including the hated *macinato*, and issued a decree dividing the communal land among those who had fought in the war of liberation or their heirs. Acute disorder followed as the peasants, who were quite uninterested in following Garibaldi to the mainland, tried to get possession of those lands which had been illegally acquired since 1812. Political revolution Garibaldi was prepared to lead; social revolution went far beyond what he could accept. The guns of his troops were turned on the peasantry at Bronte on 4 August 1860, and many Sicilians began to think that annexation to Piedmont offered the best path to stability and security.

Cavour found himself in a very difficult position as a consequence of Garibaldi's success. France began to press for a six-month armistice between Naples and Sicily and, since Garibaldi showed no sign of being prepared to delay his vault to the mainland, the spectre of French intervention loomed. Moreover, the king was busily undermining his premier's policy. Victor Emmanuel wrote to Garibaldi passing on as a 'suggestion' the proposal that all Bourbon troops would leave Sicily if Garibaldi undertook not to land on the mainland, but also sent a secret note advising him to reply in terms of respect but to state that if he did not act against the mainland Italian patriots would call him to account. What worried Cavour most was that Garibaldi would simply refuse to give up the dictatorship he had assumed and would extend it to Naples.

Cavour tried to collapse the Naples government from inside, but failed. He then ordered the navy indirectly to impede Garibaldi's crossing as much as possible, but his quarry crossed the Straits of Messina on 18/19 August 1860 at the third attempt. On 7 September, after brushing aside feeble resistance, Garibaldi entered Naples to a rapturous reception; two days earlier, as Cavour had feared, he announced that before annexation he intended to liberate Rome – a move which was bound to result in French intervention. Cavour now showed the extent of his diplomatic skills, persuading Napoleon III to agree to Piedmont's occupying Umbria and the Marches to suppress a manufactured insurrection on condition that Rome remained inviolable. Piedmontese troops crossed the papal frontier on 11 September and in eighteen days the campaign was over. It had brought royal armies to the northern border of the kingdom of Naples in one bound.

On 1 October Garibaldi's armies defeated 30,000 Bourbon troops at the battle of the Volturno. However, at the moment of military success Garibaldi was about to meet political defeat. Cavour recalled parliament the following day and it consented to annexation of the Bourbon kingdom by royal decree after a plebiscite. That plebiscite was duly held nineteen days later. On the mainland 1,312,366 voted (79.5 per cent of those entitled to do so), of whom 1,302,064 chose union with Italy 'one and indivisible'; in Sicily 432,720 voted (75.2 per cent of those eligible), of whom 432,053 voted for union. In neither case were voters given the choice of a separate kingdom, as had happened in Emilia and Tuscany. Outmanoeuvred, Garibaldi met Victor Emmanuel II at Teano on 26 October 1860 and handed the Bourbon kingdom over to him. According to some sources the king responded by greeting 'my best friend'; according to others he merely replied 'thank you'. The last Bourbon troops in Sicily surrendered when the fortress of Messina fell on 13 March 1861, and eleven days later the last mainland garrison surrendered.

THE PROBLEMS OF A PARLIAMENTARY MONARCHY

The kingdom of Italy formally came into existence on 17 March 1861 when Victor Emmanuel II adopted the new title. Its problems were immense. A backward economy was based predominantly on agriculture, and its capacity to create wealth was thus extremely limited. The mass of the population lived in conditions of abject poverty and ignorance – a survey in 1864 estimated that of some 26 million people no more than 12 per cent were literate – and had few loyalties beyond those to family and village. And a large slice of the new kingdom showed the utmost reluctance to knuckle under and accept Piedmontese rule: between

1861 and 1865 a civil war was waged in the south against large bands of brigands and by the time it was over tens of thousands of civilians had died. That war was largely social in origin, having much to do with the government's slowness in distributing demesne lands and the failure of the peasantry to get much of a share, but many saw it as a political fact which indicated that Italy was not yet ready for full unification.

The structure of future government control presented major difficulties. Should Italy be centralized like France, or decentralized like the United States, or should it occupy some indeterminate midpoint? At first it was proposed that the country should be divided up into some seven or eight large regions ruled by governors nominated by the crown, but this proposal was criticized on a variety of grounds: the regions varied widely in size, some were not historical entities, and the south was too big to be a single region of this kind. Behind these criticisms lay the fear that regions might become autonomist and also, perhaps, the spectre of the 'over-mighty governor'. By the end of 1861 the regional idea had collapsed, to be replaced by the introduction of prefects to control provinces – larger in number but considerably smaller in size. This structure was embodied in the laws on legislative and administrative unification of March 1865 which confirmed the crown's power to nominate mayors as well as to appoint prefects and which gave central government many of the responsibilities formerly held by the provinces, such as the building and maintenance of roads. For Lombardy in particular the new structure meant a notable loss of autonomy. Church and state were formally separated in the Italian Civil Code, introduced in January 1866, which recognized the legality of a purely civil marriage.

The electoral system, introduced in 1861, set up colleges which returned 443 deputies to the lower chamber of parliament; members of the upper chamber, or Senate, were nominated by the king. To qualify, electors had to have reached the age of 25, be able to read and write, and pay at least 40 *lire* in direct taxes each year. These restrictions produced an electorate of 418,696, or less than 2 per cent of the population. The contrast with the plebiscites of 1860 is a striking one. Even this minute 'political nation' took little interest in national politics: in elections held on 27 January 1861 only 239,583 bothered to vote. Perhaps more important was the general election of October 1865 which saw the rise of a constitutional left which rejected Mazzinian ideas of republican federation and preferred to work for reform within the framework of a constitutional monarchy. The moderate conservatives (known as the *Destra* or Right) won that election but the Left returned some 120 deputies and eleven years later this group toppled the heirs to Cavour.

Rome and Venetia still lay outside the control of the new kingdom. On 25 March 1861 Cavour stated publicly that Rome must be the capital of Italy, but added that the new kingdom must go there with French support. The seemingly impassable barrier to this was that the papacy would not relinquish its temporal power. The politicians sought to solve the Roman question by diplomacy, while Victor Emmanuel II and Garibaldi wanted to solve both questions by force. The king encouraged Garibaldi to think of another expedition, perhaps to Hungary, out of which Italy might snatch Venetia; but when, at Marsala in July 1862, the hero of partisan warfare announced '*O Roma, o morte*' (Rome or death) the king hastily published a proclamation disapproving of the undertaking. Garibaldi shook off the authorities and reached the southern mainland but was stopped by Italian troops at Aspromonte on 29 August 1862. How to loosen the Austrian grip on the north-east, and how to reconcile France to the disappearance of a papal state which Napoleon III had restored in 1849, remained problems of seemingly irresolvable difficulty. When, in 1864, Napoleon III supported the transfer of the Italian capital from Turin to Florence, he did so in the belief that it signalled the abandonment of the Roman aspirations.

THE WAR OF 1866

The unexpected catalyst which readjusted the international balance of power in such a way as to allow Italy to complete her unification came in the form of Prussian ambition. Early in July

1865 Bismarck, the chancellor of Prussia, sounded out the Italian government on its attitude in the event of a war between Prussia and Austria. At this stage France was unwilling to give its blessing to such a war but when, in February 1866, Bismarck asked for a military alliance with Italy preparatory to war Napoleon III changed his mind. On 18 April a defensive—offensive alliance was signed which bound Italy to declare war on Austria as soon as Prussia started hostilities, in return for which she was to receive Venetia and the province of Mantua – which had been withheld from her in 1859. Since neither partner wholly trusted the other, the treaty was given a three-month life span. Vienna sought to break the partnership by offering to cede Venetia to France, who would then pass it on to Victor Emmanuel, if Italy backed out of her agreement. Italy could not fall in with this scheme because Napoleon III would only hand over Venetia on condition that Italy accepted Papal rule in Rome. Victor Emmanuel II was – as always – keen to fight and Italy had no real choice but to follow him.

The war which began on 20 June 1866 was characterized by a lack of co-ordination between Italy and Prussia and by suspicions and rivalries among the Italian high command which destroyed military cohesion. Four days after hostilities had begun, the Italian army met defeat at the battle of Custozza. The Prussian army did rather better at Königgrätz on 3 July, and five days later Bismarck began to discuss terms with his defeated opponent. Italy refused to halt her operations, hoping to seize the Trentino, into which Garibaldi's units were penetrating with considerable success. On 20 July it was the turn of the Italian navy to suffer humiliation at the hands of Austria in the battle of Lissa, and next day Prussia announced a truce. Unable to carry on the fight alone Italy abandoned hopes of gaining the Trentino for the time being and gave up the war. By the terms of the Peace of Vienna, signed on 3 October 1866, Austria ceded Venetia to Italy and recognized the new kingdom; and in a plebiscite held eighteen days later 647,486 Venetians voted for union with the Italian kingdom and only 60 against. With Rome the only outstanding item on the agenda, Italy could now loosen links with France which many had found humiliating – albeit necessary.

Domestic problems temporarily pushed the Roman question into the wings after the war of 1866. Italy's financial situation was desperate, and measures had to be agreed to cut back the massive national debt which unification had incurred: these included the general introduction of the *macinato* from January 1869. There was also a continuing problem of internal disorder, exemplified by the revolt of Palermo in September 1866. Sicily was fertile ground for every kind of agitator because of its traditional separatism, because the national government had gone back on its word and had sold off ecclesiastical lands instead of dividing them up by lot, and because the suppression of the convents, which was part of the anti-clerical programme, ended the charity upon which the very poorest had depended. A confused rising, in which the crowds chanted a slogan supporting the republic, the crown and the Church, lasted from 15 to 22 September, when it was crushed by the army. To keep order thereafter the government entered into informal arrangements with the Mafia.

By the spring of 1867 Garibaldi was growing restless again, and in March he began to plan an insurrection in Lazio. Almost everyone opposed this scheme except Victor Emmanuel II who covertly encouraged the 'Lion of Caprera'. The king's motives were not, however, entirely straightforward for he said privately that he intended to pursue the Garibaldini into the Papal States and 'massacre them so that not one would be left'. Despite being under observation, Garibaldi slipped away from his refuge on the island of Caprera and arrived at the Papal frontier on 23 October to take command of his waiting volunteers. An insurrection planned to take place the previous day in Rome failed, undercutting the basis of the expedition, and the arrival of French troops to protect the Pope sealed Garibaldi's fate. His volunteers were decisively beaten at the battle of Mentana on 3 November 1867, chiefly by the formidable power of the new *chassepot* rifle.

By the end of 1867 the Roman question appeared to be at an irresolvable impasse. The French stated publicly that Italy would never possess Rome and the Italians proclaimed that sooner or later it would become the capital of Italy. Conservative politicians were content to wait upon events and in July 1870 the outbreak of the Franco-Prussian war offered an opportunity. Victor Emmanuel II wanted to join in alongside the French at once, calculating that they would win and would then gratefully part with the Holy City, but was restrained by his more cautious ministers. The news of the battle of Sedan and the declaration of the Third Republic, which reached Italy on 5 September, galvanized the cabinet into action and it was decided to take Rome without delay. At 5.15 am on the morning of 20 September Italian military artillery began battering a breach in the walls of Rome at Porta Pia and by 10.10 am the battle was over. Taking the city cost the lives of forty-nine Italian soldiers and nineteen of the Papal Guard.

Unlike the three previous wars of the Risorgimento, the last act seemed drab and devoid of inspiring principle. To counteract this, plans were made for Victor Emmanuel II to arrive in triumphal procession at the heart of the new capital by way of the Roman Forum and the Via Sacra, but they came to nothing. The king finally slipped surreptitiously into Rome in December 1870 to inspect damage caused by the flooding of the Tiber. As he stepped from his carriage at the door of the Quirinale palace he turned to general La Marmora and murmured, 'At last we're here.' Appropriately, the words were uttered not in Italian but in Piedmontese.

Ideals and ambition together created a united Italy. The ideals were to be found mainly on the Left. The martyrs who died before Austrian or Neapolitan firing squads sanctified the struggle for independence. Young Italy kept ideals alive with its commitment to action; and Mazzini provided both a political ideology and a fiercely national conviction that Italy could and must come into existence. Garibaldi's military successes, and his striking personal charisma, won victories for Italy on the field and in Europe's drawing rooms. But he was both fiercely democratic and resolutely nationalistic. In 1860 these ideals could not easily be reconciled, and at Teano in November Garibaldi showed that his greater loyalty was to Italy. However, he remained wedded to democratic ideals and tinged with a vague aura of republicanism and was thus a threat to the state Cavour had established.

37

The ambition was Piedmont's, and although it was shared by Cavour and Victor Emmanuel they were the heirs to a long-standing appetite: according to cardinal Richelieu, grand-duke Charles Emmanuel I of Piedmont (1580–1630) had once told him that Italy was 'like an artichoke, which must be eaten leaf by leaf'. Cavour's contribution to the Risorgimento was to create a constitutional state which the Great Powers found tolerable and Italian patriots eventually found acceptable. In 1859 he had the skill to take advantage of the opportunity provided for him by British and French sympathy for Piedmont. Thereafter, and until his death in 1861, he had to exercise all his considerable manipulative arts to protect the infant Italy from Garibaldi, who wanted to go too far and too fast.

The Risorgimento in history

Since each of the régimes which has ruled Italy since 1870 has at some time claimed to be the true heir of the Risorgimento, the past has come to have a heightened political importance in Italy. Critics of each and all of those régimes have attacked the defects of the Italian state which was created by 1870. The result has been a lively – and at times violent – debate about the past which has usually been cast in terms of 'success' or 'failure'.

The dynastic historians of the late nineteenth century fabricated a Risorgimento in which the house of Savoy had been the standard-bearer of liberal constitutionalism, allying itself with whatever progressive forces were to hand for the greater good of the Italian people. In doing this they were merely imitating Victor Emmanuel II who by 1851 was assiduously spreading the legend of the 'liberal king' by claiming that he had personally saved the constitution in 1849 (see p. 15 above). Other legends were quickly added to the stock: for example, that Victor Emmanuel had wanted to continue fighting in July 1859 but had been overborne by Napoleon III, which was quite untrue. The early histories of the Risorgimento gilded the role played by the crown by simply omitting documents which contradicted this picture or by mistranslating foreign sources. The 'heroic Risorgimento' of the late nineteenth century was thus an easy target for attack by liberal historians of the twentieth century, who began to reveal the shortcomings of the monarchy.

This 'debunking' continued during the Fascist period. Fascism existed none too happily alongside the monarchy, and work which demonstrated the deficiencies of the house of Savoy was not discouraged. Generally, however, Fascist historiography sought to highlight the elements of power and national grandeur whilst underplaying the theme of liberty. Historians also painted the Risorgimento as a steady process of integrating the masses into the nation, culminating in Fascism. In the search for heroic figures who would justify Mussolini, Garibaldi was sometimes depicted as the forerunner of D'Annunzio, and the expedition to Sapri (see p. 22 above) was honoured as the true precursor of the March on Rome of 1922.

Harsh criticism was levelled at the Risorgimento during the 1920s and 1930s by the Italian Marxist Antonio Gramsci. Although temperamentally more disposed to the Party of Action led by Mazzini and Garibaldi than to Cavour's bourgeois moderates, Gramsci was critical of Mazzini and Garibaldi because of their failure to mobilize the rural peasant masses as the Jacobins had done at the start of the French Revolution. This *rivoluzione mancata* (missing revolution) was for Gramsci the central fact which had condemned Italy to Liberalism and then to Fascism. For him, the Party of Action had failed to develop the triad of party, programme and agitation of the rural masses which were the essentials for a successful revolution, and were thus no more than propagandists for the moderates. Gramsci's theory of betrayal took the example of the February revolution of 1917 in Russia too readily as an ideal type. Socialist historians attacked him on the grounds that the natural alliance of industrial proletariat which leads, and rural proletariat which follows and supports, which alone could have produced a historical turnaround, was impossible because of the backwardness of industrialization in Italy.

The picture of the Risorgimento as 'the revolution of the rich' is hard to controvert, but since the Second World War Gramsci's charge of failure has been rebutted by neo-conservative historians on two main grounds: first, that an alliance between bourgeoisie and peasantry, which did – as we have seen – occasionally come about, could never have been made the permanent basis of unification since the two groups sought different aims and were therefore bound to break apart once one partner had achieved those aims; and secondly, that in any case a peasant revolution, had it taken place, would have struck at the landed bourgeoisie whose accumulation of capital was an essential foundation of the industrial and economic take-off of the 1890s. Without the surplus produced by a landless or tied peasantry this take-off could not have happened. These views are still highly controversial especially on the political left.

Non-Italian historians have often stressed the crucial role played by the Great Powers in the unification of Italy. Whilst favourable international circumstances were an essential prerequisite for the successful completion of the Risorgimento, they only permitted Piedmont to unify Italy but did not compel her to do so. The motive forces have to be sought within Italy and among Italians. They were, as has been seen, complex: various kinds and degrees of patriotism and idealism acted alongside dynastic calculation, sometimes amicably and sometimes not. Social and economic forces were led – and sometimes pushed – by individuals of widely varying character: Mazzini, Cavour, Garibaldi, Victor Emmanuel, Pisacane and Pallavicino all contributed to the final outcome but were not all in accord with one another. Where contemporaries were often in conflict we cannot expect historians to arrive at any comfortable consensus. So complex was the struggle for unification, and so strong are the emotions which it can still arouse, that its history will continue to be rewitten by each generation and from every political perspective.

Suggested reading

Place of publication is London unless otherwise stated; paperbacks are marked*

Recently, two fine general surveys of early nineteenth-century Italy have been published which complement one another well: Stuart Woolf, *A History of Italy 1700–1860: The Social Constraints of Political Change* (Methuen, 1979)*; and Harry Hearder, *Italy in the Age of the Risorgimento* (Longman, 1983)*. Some of the main documents of the period have been edited and translated in Denis Mack Smith, *The Making of Italy, 1796–1870* (Macmillan, 1968), and Derek Beales, *The Risorgimento and the Unification of Italy* (Allen & Unwin, 1971)*. A more specialized study is Denis Mack Smith, *A History of Sicily: Modern Sicily after 1713* (Chatto & Windus, 1968).

Of the leading protagonists of the Risorgimento, Mazzini has been given sympathetic treatment in E. E. Y. Hales, *Mazzini and the Secret Societies: The Making of a Myth* (Eyre & Spottiswoode, 1956); and the same author has also written a biography of Pius IX, *Pio Nono: A Study in European Politics and Religion in the Nineteenth Century* (Eyre & Spottiswoode, 1956). The most recent biography of Garibaldi is Jasper Ridley, *Garibaldi* (Constable, 1974). Denis Mack Smith, *Victor Emmanuel, Cavour and the Risorgimento* (Oxford, Oxford University Press, 1971) is invaluable. The role of Cavour is examined in detail in a recent biography also by Denis Mack Smith, *Cavour* (Weidenfeld & Nicolson, 1985; Methuen 1985*). Clara Maria Lovett, *Carlo Cattaneo and the Politics of the Risorgimento* (The Hague, Martinus Nijhoff, 1972), examines the career and thought of an important if lesser figure.

Kent Roberts Greenfield, *Economics and Liberalism in the Risorgimento: A Study of Nationalism in Lombardy, 1814–1848* (Baltimore, Johns

Hopkins University Press, 1965), analyses one aspect of the economic roots of the Risorgimento. Two books deal with important aspects of the revolution of 1848 in Italy: Paul Ginsborg, *Daniele Manin and the Venetian Revolution of 1848–49* (Cambridge, Cambridge University Press, 1979), and Alan Sked, *The Survivor of the Habsburg Empire: Radetzky, the Imperial Army and the Class War, 1848* (Longman, 1979). The role of the Italian National Society, often overlooked, is examined in Raymond Grew, *A Sterner Plan for Unity: The Italian National Society in the Risorgimento* (Princeton, Princeton University Press, 1963). Gramsci's case for a 'missing revolution' is explained in J. M. Cammett, *Antonio Gramsci and the Origins of Italian Communism* (Stanford, Stanford University Press 1967).

Four other Lancaster Pamphlets contain material related to that discussed here. Martin Blinkhorn, *Mussolini and Fascist Italy*, examines a subsequent period in Italian history; and J. M. MacKenzie, *The Partition of Africa*, places Italian colonial interests in their international setting. The international context of Mussolini's diplomacy is presented in two pamphlets by Ruth Henig, *Versailles and After 1919–1933* and *The Origins of the Second World War*.